Keep reading and ya'll be succeeding!

Hysterical Rhymes
and How You Can Rhyme Too!

by Derek Taylor Kent
with illustrations by Travis Hanson

Simon and the Solar System (ages 4-9)
El Perro con Sombrero (ages 3-8)
El Perro con Sombrero meets
Los Gatos con Gelatos (ages 3-8)
Doggy Claus/Perro Noel (ages 3-8)
The Scary School Series (ages 7-12, 4-book series)
The Whimsical World Coloring Book (ages 3+)

Counting Sea Life with the Little Seahorse (ages 2-4)
Principal Mikey (ages 7-12)
My Homework Ate My Dog! (ages 8-12)
Kubrick's Game (ages 13+)
The Grossest Picture Book Ever (ages 3-9)
Dinosaur Derby (ages 3-8)
The Leaning Tower of Pizza (ages 3-8)

www.WhimsicalWorldBooks.com
www.DerekTaylorKent.com

Text ©2021 by Derek Taylor Kent
Illustrations ©2021 by Derek Taylor Kent
All rights reserved.
Library of Congress Control Number: 2021922087
Kent, Derek Taylor
Hysterical Rhymes and How You Can Rhyme Too!/Derek Taylor Kent : Illustrations by Travis Hanson
140 pages 7,5x9,25 inches
ISBN (Hardcover) 978-1-949213-36-2
ISBN (Softcover) 978-1-949213-39-3

For information on book purchases, please contact the Whimsical World sales department at info@WhimsicalWorldBooks.com

First Edition 2021 – Designed by Travis Hanson
Printed in China

 Hi! I'm the author, Derek Taylor Kent, and let me tell you something…

I LOOOOOVE POETRY!

Please don't beat me up just yet. I know that I have one of those real 'punchable' faces, but just give me a minute to explain.

I've been writing funny poems since I was ten years old. My best friend, Ryan, and I liked to write stories, skits, and poems to make each other laugh. At some point we realized that for some reason when our stories rhymed, they were ten times funnier.

For instance, you could say:

I went to the market, slipped on some spilled juice, and fell on my butt.

And that's kind of funny. But, watch what happens when you write it like this:

I went to the market, and then you know what?
I slipped on some juice and I fell on my butt.

Did the second one make you chuckle? Exactly. I don't know the science behind how our brain works that makes rhyming funny, but I know that when I was ten years old, I loved being able to make my friends laugh. To this day, I still love making friends, family, and kids all around the world laugh with the ridiculous and (usually) absurd things that pop into my head.

Artists use clay, painters use paint, and poets use language to create beauty, search for truth, and sometimes make us roll on the ground in hysterics. As I share with you some of the silliest poems I've ever written, I'll also tell you a bit about how I wrote them so you can create you own funny poems because spreading joy and laughter is one of the greatest gifts you can give to the world.

Okay you can beat me up now.

50 Ridiculous Rhymes
part 1

There's a Dog in My Lap

There's a dog in my lap
For that's where he must nap,
Even though there's a bed that I bought him.
It's just the right size
But the pup never tries!
On my thighs is the one place you'll spot him.

When I leave for the bus,
Oh, he makes quite a fuss,
Then he waits all day long by the door.
When I get home to feed him
Before I can greet him,
He's back in my lap for some more!

He's stuck there like glue,
There's not much I can do.
At the table we lack all decorum.
I could push him or shove him
But the truth is I love him
So much, there's no better place for him.

The Hairiest Beast

What is the hairiest beast of them all?
Is the beast big or is the beast small?
Does it stomp through the forest and hide in a cave?
Or lurch through the desert in need of a shave?
Does it migrate in winter or live in the trees?
Or stand where its hair can flow free in the breeze?

What is the hairiest beast of them all?
Is the beast short or is the beast tall?
Does it feast on the critters that fly in its fur?
Or hunt like a lion, then happily purr?
Does it howl at the moon? Does it roar like a bear?
Does it cry out in anger through all of its hair?

What beast is most hairy? It must have a name.
I wondered and wondered…
then one day it came!
It was wet! It was stinky! It filled me with dread!
I yelled to my sister to hide 'neath the bed.
I discovered the beast that was truly most hairy

When it emerged from the bathroom…

    My Uncle Larry.

How Do I Rhyme?

Rhyming is one of the classic characteristics of poetry. Some poems are written in what's called free verse, which does not rhyme, but most poems rhyme in one way or another.

Before you start writing a poem, or shortly after you get started, it's important to figure out what your rhyme scheme is going to be.

The poem you just read, *The Hairiest Beast,* is written in rhyming couplets. That's where two lines rhyme with one another in succession.

What is the hairiest beast of them all?
Is the beast big or is the beast small?
Does it stomp through the forest and hide in a cave?
Or lurch through the desert in need of a shave?

You can describe it as AA, BB, CC, DD etc. A is one type of rhyme: all and small. B, is the next rhyme cave and shave.

THERE'S A DOG IN MY LAP had a different rhyme scheme: AABCCB / DDFGGF

The / indicates a new stanza. A stanza in poetry is like a paragraph in a book. Basically, it's a chunk of text that's meant to go together and convey one idea before moving on to the next. Here's the first stanza for There's a Dog in My Lap with the rhyme scheme written next to it.

A	There's a dog in my lap
A	For that's where he must nap,
B	Even though there's a bed that I bought him.
C	It's just the right size
C	But the pup never tries!
B	On my thighs is the one place you'll spot him.

Pretty easy, right?

Besides rhyming couplets, another common rhyme is alternate rhymes that look like ABAB / CDCD. You can also have internal rhymes where words within a line rhyme with each other. You can have enclosed rhymes where the rhymes work from the outside in! Like this: ABCDDCBA.

There's lots of room for creativity when coming up with a rhyme scheme, and in this book, you'll find many different types of them. Most of them are classic ones that I like best, but sometimes I like to experiment and try different combinations. When I come up with a weird scheme like AABA CCBC, I wonder if they've ever been done before!

There are also different kinds of rhymes. You can have an exact rhyme like: ham, jam, tram, ma'am, ram.

But you can also use near rhymes, such as ham and plan, castle and dazzle, and one you're about to read in an upcoming poem, butchery and cookery. I checked and I don't think those words have ever rhymed in a poem before! In near rhymes, usually just the ending vowel sounds rhymes, but in exact rhymes, the vowel and consonant sounds rhyme.

Typically I will try to use an exact rhyme in my poems, but sometimes the right rhyme just doesn't exist for what I need to say and a near rhyme works best. The sheer creativity of a near rhyme can often make it amusing. When I want to rhyme a really tough word like butchery, there aren't a wide array of options, but that's when I enjoy the challenge of poetry the most.

It doesn't even have to be just one word rhyming with one word. You can have your first word be *fortress* and you rhyme it with *court dress*. You can even take a really long word like Disneyland and rhyme it with: his flea band.

While there is absolutely nothing wrong with using simple rhymes in a poem, the more you write, the more those simple rhymes like day and way will feel too easy and you'll want the challenge of more complex rhymes, perhaps ones that have never been done before.

As you read this book, see if you start to notice any rhymes you may not have ever read before. I encourage you to write down your favorites. At the end of the book, I'll give you a fun challenge for them.

Helicopter 4 Sale

Who wants my chopper? I'm a seller!
It's only missing one propeller.
Plus a few more parts (perhaps eight or nine).
Just never land it and you'll be fine.

Who Invented the Cupcake?

Of all of the genius that ever existed,
There's one who I don't think I've ever seen listed.
Not Edison, Hamilton, Einstein or Blake,
— Amelia Simmons! Inventor of cupcake!

A cake in a cup! Not a dish or a pan
Or a sheet or a rack or a pot or a can.
Whose idea was so bright that it outshone the sun?
Who thought of a way to make birthdays more fun?

I'll tell you who! It's my favorite maker—
Amelia Simmons. America's Baker!

Just twenty years after our great independence
She realized our food deserved worldwide acceptance.
"Our baking's not British and neither's our butchery,
So I'll write a book on American cookery!"

American Cookery sold millions of prints,
And cupcakes have popped up in bakeries since.
So when eating a cupcake, take time and give thanks
To a woman whose genius no other outranks.

A cake in a cup. What idea could be greater?
Remember Amelia — the cupcake creator.

How Long Should a Poem Be?

The answer to this one is easy. As long as it needs to be!

Some poems, like the epic Dante's Inferno, are as long as entire novels. It can take a grownup days and days to read it! Some poems are super-duper short, like the *Helicopter for Sale* poem you just read. I once met a poet named Aram Sorayan who liked to write one-word poems. My favorite one was just: Lighght.

What does it mean? I guess that there's a lot of light.

Some poetry forms have a strict number of lines or syllables that must be adhered to. For instance Haikus are always three lines of:

Five syllables
Seven syllables
Five syllables

One of my favorite haikus is:

The falling flower
I saw drift back to the branch
Was a butterfly.

For me, I like to keep my poems as brief as possible without any extra filler, but sometimes, especially when I'm telling a story, a poem gets so long it becomes its own book. A few poems in this book almost became children's books of their own, but weren't quite long enough.

In the end, your poem is your poem, so you can make it as long or as short as you want it to be. A perfect four-line poem can be just as moving, powerful, or hilarious as a ten-page poem if it's written well.

Narwhal

I know all about the narwhal.
There's a poster pinned on our wall.

They're the unicorns of the sea
And their horn is sensory.

Other whales think they're the oddball.
They're just jealous of that rod, y'all!

The World's Craziest Sandwich

It's very nice to meet you.
You may call me Danny Dandrich,
And I am the creator
Of the world's most crazy sandwich.
If you've never tried my sandwich, well,
That's really quite a shame.
I'll teach you how to make it and
Your life won't be the same.

Begin with bread, your favorite kind,
The type and brand don't matter.
Then place two slices flat upon
Your biggest, widest platter.

Now add a scoop of tuna
And a single slice of turkey.
Then throw on a banana
And a strip of beefy jerky.
Now pile on the onions
And don't skimp on avocado.
Then pour a cup of gravy
With some fresh pollo asado.

Now add a slab of bacon
And just half a Christmas ham,
A square of jiggly Jell-O
And a jar of gooey jam.
Don't you dare forget the pizza
And a heap of mashed potato.
To keep it healthy let's toss in
Some lettuce and tomato.

Is there cheese? Oh honey, please,
There's gouda, goat and grana.
There's mozzarella, cheddar, and some
Crema Mexicana.

Now top it off with peppers
And a deboned roasted chicken.
Finish with spaghetti
And then put a real long pick in.

Toast it with a blowtorch
Then the sandwich is completed.
The problem is I haven't found
A way to actually eat it.

My Bike Beyond Belief

I love to ride my bike to school.
I can't wait till I leave.
Because I have a special bike
That you would not believe.

As soon as I unhook it from
A post in my backyard,
It tells me what the weather is
And if it rains, how hard.

Then after it has garnished me
With every bit of news,
An arm pops out from underneath
That ties and shines my shoes.

And wait til I sit on the seat,
The wonders cannot hide!
I think it does a thousand things
I have not even tried!

The first thing that I do is push
A button by the horn.
A creature then appears to me
In holographic form.

The creature's a professor
From a star not very bright.
It looks at all my homework
And makes sure I did it right.

As I pedal down the street,
Let's say the bullies have no chance.
Whoever tries to chase me
Gets knocked over by a lance.

And if the street is flooding
Well, my bike cannot get wet.
But that's no cause to worry
And I haven't worried yet.

For when I say "Propeller mode"
The bike turns into drone.
I'm sure you've walked and drove to school,
But have you ever flown?

I park my bike, it tells me bye
And keeps my lunch bag warm.
If thieves attempt to steal it,
Hives of angry bees will swarm!

If you ever care to ask me,
"Where'd you get, Val Silvassa?"
The most I can divulge is that
My mommy works for NASA.

Millie Maroney

Some people climb very tall mountains.
That requires great training and practice and skills,
But I don't have time for such arduous outings,
I'm Millie Maroney – the climber of hills!

I don't care for ropes and I don't abide rocks.
I don't like to sweat and I hate to get chills.
I cringe at the feeling of sand in my socks,
And I don't need to risk any backbreaking spills.

That's why I love hills. I've got lots in my town.
Each time I run up, oh the places it fills!
The only thing better is running back down,
But I never tumble like Jacks or like Jills.

I yelp and I leap when I reach a hill's crest.
Just minutes of effort for infinite thrills!
Yes, I know no one else is so nearly impressed,
But I'm Millie Maroney – the climber of hills.

Ryan, Ryan, Chicken Fryin'

Ryan, Ryan, Chicken Fryin'
Loves to fry and I'm not lyin'.
He's the king, though not so royal,
King of frying fowl in oil!

Ryan, Ryan, Chicken Fryin'
Doctor said, "Guess what? You're dyin'.
If you fry once more with oil,
You'll end up down deep in soil."

Ryan, Ryan, Chicken Fryin'
No-Fry cookin' he was tryin'.
Made himself a chicken boil.
It was awful with no oil!

Ryan, Ryan, Chicken Fryin'
Lots of cookbooks he was spyin'.
Baked a chicken wrapped in foil.
Still no match for deep fried oil!

Ryan, Ryan, Chicken Fryin'
Un-fried chicken had him cryin'.
It got crispy in a broil—
Not as crispy drenched in oil.

Ryan, Ryan, Chicken Fryin'
No more chicken he was buyin'.
What he had all went to spoil.
Not worth cooking with no oil.

Ryan, Ryan, no more cheer,
Doctor said, "You're in the clear!"
Now he fries with so much oil,
It was worth the pain and toil.

How Do I Decide What to Write About?

This is a really great question. Sometimes ideas seem to come real easily. Other times, it can feel like the hardest thing in the world.

One great way to come up with an idea for a poem is to draw on your own emotions. A poet will often write a poem in order to share a strong emotion that they are feeling, and hopefully elicit the same emotion in the reader. In this way, the reader and the poet share a special connection.

If you're feeling sad, it can help to read a sad poem and know that others have also spent days crying their eyes out.

What do you have big feelings about? Do you love someone extra special in your life? You can try writing a poem about what that love feels like. You can write a poem for that person that shares why you love them so much.

You can also find ideas simply by looking at what's around you and maybe give it more attention than you normally would. Have you ever stopped and really looked closely at a beautiful flower? What if you took a magnifying glass and looked at every single speck on each petal?

Another great way to find inspiration is to read as much as you can. My biggest inspirations for my children's poetry are Dr. Seuss, Ogden Nash, Shel Silverstein, Edgar Alan Poe, and Robert Louis Stevenson. You've probably heard of a couple of them, but if you find that you like reading poetry, you should look up the others.

As you read more poems in this book, you will notice that there are several poems about dogs. That's because I grew up with dogs and today my dog, Zander, is my best buddy and constant source of humor and inspiration.

I also love writing poems about my beautiful wife, about growing up, about funny things I notice in life, and about all the different kinds of creatures in the animal kingdom because I love animals so much.

One of the biggest feelings I've had to deal with my entire life is fear. When I was a kid, I had a crippling fear of both rollercoasters and talking to girls. In this next poem, you'll see what those fears were like in my head and also get a little hint about how I was eventually able to overcome them.

I Do Not Want to Ride that Coaster

I know that before I proclaimed I was brave,
But now Lee regrets being such a big boaster.
Will this be the day I am sent to my grave?
I do not want to ride on that coaster.

There's too many loops and that drop looks so steep,
Lee could be tossed like a toast out of toaster!
Those corkscrews and turns would make any man weep.
There's no way, no how, I will ride on that coaster.

Uh oh…

The girl that I like just showed up here by chance.
She says, "Are you going to ride on that ride, Lee?
It looked kind of scary to me at first glance,
But maybe I'd ride it if you sat beside me."

My heart gave me strength, like a standing ovation.
I said, "Lee's not scared of some silly old coaster."
I guess being brave needs the right motivation.
And the photo we got is my favorite poster.

But Mom!

You must go out and exercise
You must go out and play
You must go out and run around
And get some sun today.

But Mom, there is a blizzard
And the sky is dark and grey.
I could go out, but honestly,
I think it's best I stay.

Fine, she said, then stay inside
And go play with your sister.
But Mom, I am an *only* kid,
Unless I somehow missed her.

Fine, she said, then go to bed.
I'll bring your night-night cup.
But Mom, it's only 8 am
I barely just woke up.

Fine, she said, then read a book.
Now that's an indoor deed!
But mom, I'm only five years old.
I haven't learned to read.

Fine she said, I'm giving up
Today will be your turn.
Mom, I said, let's have a talk,
There's much for you to learn.

Porcupines

The porcupine's a ball of spikes
So if boy finds a girl he likes,
He must resist her pleas and tugs
Or be impaled when first he hugs.

Who is Naming Animals?

Whoever's naming animals is wrong and must be blamed.
I've learned about so many that are not what they are named!

A guinea pig is not a pig.
A prairie dog is not a dog.
A killer whale is not a whale.
A groundhog is no hog.

A mole-rat's neither mole nor rat. A bearcat's neither bear nor cat.
A flying fox is a just a bat, but wombats are not bats, they're rats!

A honey badger's not a badger.
An electric eel is not an eel.
A dragonfly's not fly nor dragon,
But still can make me squeal.

A kangaroo rat's not a rat, oh, and not a kangaroo.
Whoever's naming animals must not have thought this through.

A horseshoe crab is not a crab.
A camel spider's not a spider.
A flying squirrel doesn't fly,
It's actually a glider.

Whoever named the Sea Lion was hardly even tryin'.
A koala bear is not a bear. I wish that I were lyin'!

The horny toad is not a toad
It's actually a lizard.
The mantis shrimp is not a shrimp,
It looks more like a wizard!

A silverfish is not a fish and crayfish ain't fish too.
A praying mantis doesn't pray, but preys on bugs, it's true!

The red panda may be red-ish
But it's certainly no panda.
To call that one a panda was just
Panda propaganda!

I do not mean to brag, so do not think I am a snob,
But if I were naming animals, I'd do a better job.

What are Rhythm and Meter?

Have you ever noticed that most poems, and especially ones you've been reading in this book, seem to have a distinct rhythm to them? Almost like they are songs with a beat you can tap your foot to?

This rhythm is the overall tempo or pace at which the poem unfolds. Oftentimes funny poems have a fast pace that aids in the humor, while more serious poems have a slower more deliberate meter. Do the words tend to be short or long? Are the lines of each stanza lengthy or short? All of these factor into determining the rhythm.

Notice the difference in rhythm between these two previous poems:

Of all of the genius that ever existed,
There's one who I don't think I've ever seen listed.
Not Edison, Hamilton, Einstein or Blake,
        Amelia Simmons! Inventor of cupcake!

Vs.

Ryan, Ryan, Chicken Fryin'
Loved to fry and I'm not lyin'.
He's the king, though not so royal,
King of frying fowl in oil!

The second one has a much faster rhythm, doesn't it?

Meter is the pattern of stressed and unstressed syllables. To scan a poem is to decipher the metrical pattern by annotating it (marking it up) and figuring out the meter and what type of poem it is. It's one of the most important things to understand if you want to become a master of verse.

The formal way of annotating meter is to write a slash (/) over the top of a stressed syllable and a little cuphook (˘) over an unstressed syllable. The cuphook symbol doesn't appear on most keyboards, though, so here we will just capitalize the stressed syllables.

The following text is from Dr. Seuss's *And to Think that I Saw it on Mulberry Street* and *If I Ran the Circus*. These examples show lines of what is called anapest meter, where there are two unstressed syllables followed by a stressed syllable. All of Dr. Seuss's storybooks follow this same meter.

Now that is a story that no one can beat
And to think that I saw it on Mulberry Street!
now THAT is a STOR-y that NO one can BEAT.
and to THINK that i SAW it on MUL-berr-y STREET.

In all the whole town the most wonderful spot
Is behind Sneelock's store in the big vacant lot.
in ALL the whole TOWN the most WON-der-ful SPOT
is be-HIND snee-lock's STORE in the BIG vac-ant LOT.

Sometimes I even like to think about it like a drum beat: da-da-DUM-da-da-DUM-da-da-DUM-da-da-DUM.

A lot of poets don't like to be constrained by meter or rhyme, and only write in free verse. For me, though, writing free verse would be like playing tennis without a net. Sure, it would be a lot easier, but it would also be a lot less challenging and a lot less fun. There's some free verse that I absolutely love, but in my opinion, you should become a master of form before you start to break the rules, otherwise you won't really understand why breaking the rules was the best choice for your poem.

Another common pattern is called an iamb, where there is one stressed syllable followed by a stressed one ˘ / - da-DUM da-DUM da-DUM. That's called the iambic meter. All of Shakespeare's sonnets are written this way. Here's a line from one:

Shall I compare thee to a summer's day?
shall I com-PARE thee TO a SUMM-ers DAY?

A stressed syllable and its companion unstressed syllable(s) together are called a foot. A foot may be a single word, or may be made up of two words or even parts of two words.

The next few poems you will read have different rhythm and meters to them. See if you can figure them out!

If you Try to Give My Dog a Bath

If you try to give my dog a bath
The first step is the chase.
He'll hide so well you'll search for days
To find his hiding place.

If you catch my dog, hold tight your grip.
The next step is upstairs.
He'll beg and start to offer you
His earthly doggy wares.

"You need a bone? This one's for you!
Just put me on all fours.
You need a toy? I've got a few.
Just free me and it's yours!"

If you try to give my dog a bath,
You may not meet your goal.
He'll push a button on his tag
That summons Bath Patrol.

A helicopter soon appears.
A ladder lowers down.
My dog leaps out the window,
And it flies him far from town.

But you have to give my dog a bath
So pack your bags and trunks.
After many months you'll find him
In the mountains with the monks.

You might think that you've caught him
When you bind his legs with tape.
But this pup is like Houdini,
He's a master of escape!

If you try to give my dog a bath
The mission will take years.
You'll track him with a treasure map
Through jungles full of fears.

One day you'll finally come across
A temple made of bone.
After getting through his booby traps
You'll find him on his throne.

If you try to give my dog a bath,
Bring seafood to his nose.
If you think that you outsmarted him,
There's one more trick he knows.

You tie him to your trusty leash.
The plane awaits outside.
That's when a thousand dogs appear
Who will not let this slide.

If you try to give my dog a bath
You should know what you're confronting.
They chase you throwing darts and spears —
It's you those hounds are hunting!

Quick, fly away, and don't look back,
Then cuff him to your wrist.
He'll offer you his stores of gold,
But still you must resist!

You made it back! The quest is done.
You drag him to the tub.
You fill it up with water
And prepare a sponge to scrub.

As you wash away the years of dirt
The water turns to black.
You finally gave my dog a bath,
And now you're in our pack.

As you dry him he'll be smiling,
So you'll give his head a pat.
He'll give your face a lick and say,
"You're right, I needed that!"

What Would It Sound Like?

What would it sound like
If something strange happened
And everyone suddenly sneezed?

That's 8 billion sneezes
On all seven continents!
Would you be scared or be pleased?

What would it smell like
If something strange happened
And everyone suddenly farted?

That's 8 billion farters
From 200 countries!
Earth might smell so bad I'd depart it.

Stuffies

How many stuffies is too many stuffies?
A dozen? A hundred? A thousand? A million?
Well, that's a trick question. There's never too many!
And Lenny collected them all by the billion.

It started out simply with one little penguin,
Which Lenny procured at a game at the fair.
He returned the next day and he won a stuffed lion.
The following day, an enormous stuffed bear!

It continued for weeks til the fair closed its doors.
The stuffies were piled so high on his bed,
There was no need for covers or pillows or sheets.
Lenny laid on his stuffies and loved his new spread.

Each time he went out, Lenny cried and he begged
Til he got a new stuffy to stuff in his room.
By the time he was eight, Lenny's room was so stuffy
His parents were scared it would be Lenny's tomb.

When they opened the door it was nothing but stuffies.
He burrowed inside like a mole in its den.
His mother would call out when breakfast was ready
And out popped his head like a newly hatched hen.

By the time he was ten, Lenny's parents were broke.
They shouted, "We're free! No more buying him fluffies!"
But Lenny quit school and he got a good job
And he spent every penny he earned on more stuffies!

Lenny worked hard and he loved making money.
New stuffies poured in with each raise and promotion.
The stuffies had almost filled up the whole house
And the hallways were more like a soft furry ocean.

His parents plead daily to throw some away,
But Lenny refused, he would not even share.
He had one of each stuffie that's ever been made
And he searched far and wide for the stuffies most rare.

Soon the house was so full, it became its own stuffie.
And Lenny stopped working and going outside.
With no way to get in, there was no way to find him,
And neighbors assumed that poor Lenny had died.

But every so often on long winter spells,
I will hear a soft voice cross the cold misty lamps.
The words are quite muffled, yet clear as a bell,
"Hey kiddo, you might want to just collect stamps."

The Ballad of Brady McJules

Brady McJules
Always followed the rules
So he never, not once, got in trouble.

But one day young Brady
Did quite the 180—
He ruptured his rule-loving bubble.

"From now on," he said
I will break rules instead,
Yes, not one single rule shall I follow."

"I'll scream and I'll taunt
And I'll do what I want.
If a dentist says spit, I will swallow."

His parents looked pallid
When Brady threw salad,
Insisting he get dessert first.

When nighttime arrived,
He cried, "I feel revived!
No, my bedtime shall not be coerced!"

The next day at school
Brady stood on a stool.
Then he happily slept through each class.

When picture day came
Brady gave the wrong name,
Then he rolled in nice clothes on the grass.

His mortified parents,
Named Clara and Clarence,
Were frozen in shock at his change.

Ever mild and meek
They said, "Give it a week,
Brady surely will stop acting strange."

But weeks and months passed
And his antics amassed,
Then suspensions, and finally, expelled.

He packed all he had
Said, "Goodbye, Mom and Dad,
'Cause your notions and mine never gelled."

Now with freedom complete
Brady ran to the street,
But he noticed the sign said Don't Cross.

For a moment he waited,
Then got so frustrated,
He shouted, "No sign is my boss!"

In a hospital bed
Brady's barely not dead.
Guess that bus didn't let Brady ease in.

You can break all the rules
Just like Brady McJules,
Or, just maybe, most rules have a reason.

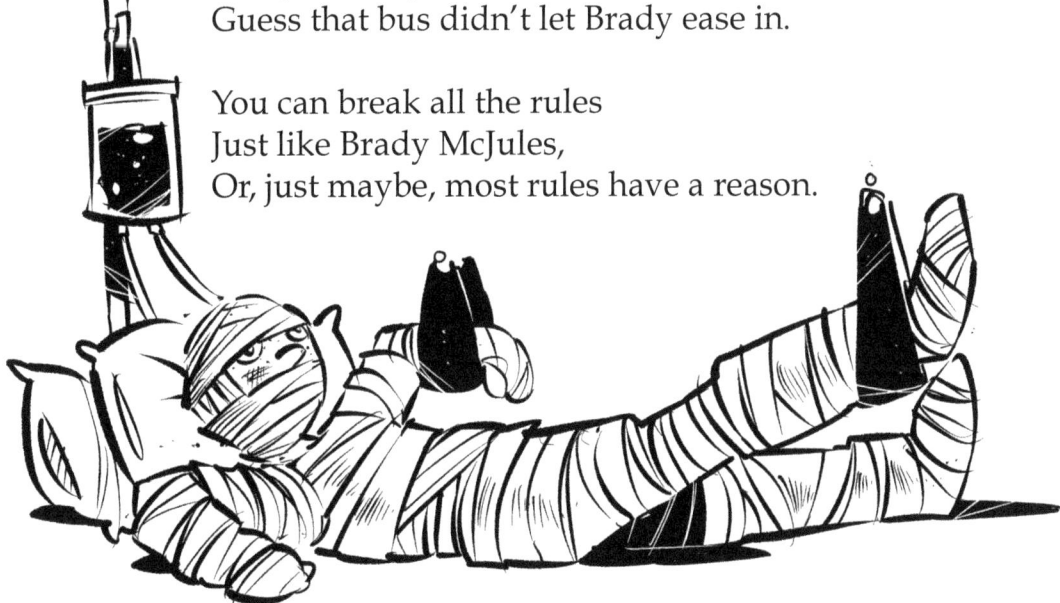

Thankful Max

My mom set down the turkey
And we held our hands in prayer.
She cleared her throat and spoke
To all the family who were there:

"Before we eat this mighty feast
And all we have in store,
Let's go around and share a bit
Of things we're thankful for."

My cousins muttered softly and their moments quickly
passed.
And when it came to me they said, "Go Max, you're next to
last."

I said, "I'm thankful for my parents
And for hamburgers with cheese.
I'm thankful for our dog
But not so thankful for her fleas.

And I'm thankful for the sunshine
And I'm thankful for the rain
And I'm thankful for my heart
And I am thankful for my brain.

And I'm thankful for my eyes
And I am thankful for my nose.
And I'm thankful for my fingers
And I'm thankful for my clothes.

I'm thankful for the freckle
On the right side of my cheek.
I'm thankful that you're patiently
Allowing me to speak.

I'm thankful for the sound
Of all our glasses when they clinked.
And dinosaurs are scary
So I'm thankful they're extinct.

I'm thankful for my friends
And I am thankful for our fridge.
And I'm thankful for koalas
And the Sydney Harbour Bridge.

And I'm thankful for the sky
And I am thankful for the ocean.
And I'm thankful for my skin
And I am thankful for skin lotion.

I'm thankful for the trees
That give us oxygen we breathe.
I'm thankful for the broccoli,
Is that so hard to believe?

I'm thankful you're my family
And I'm thankful you're all here.
And.. and…
I think that covers everything
I'm thankful for this year.

Uncle Joe said, "While I'm thankful
For our blessings shore to shore,
I'm mostly thankful Max ran out of
Things he's thankful for."

If I Had a Horse

If I had a horse
I would ride it far north,
Where the glaciers are mountains of porcelain.

Once at the North Pole
I would dig a large hole
That I'd bury my poor frozen horse in.

Bird

I found a wounded bird one night
When stepping out for air.
It hit the window in its flight
And now it's lying there.

Perhaps your wing is broken, yes?
Just chirp the word or weep.
And why were you not in your nest?
The night is meant for sleep.

I'll take you in and nurse you back
To health til you can fly.
And once you hit the air, keep track.
Please visit by and by.

How Do I Figure Out a Poem's Meaning?

This is another really great question.

When I'm trying to figure out the meaning of a poem, I break it down into three easy steps, which I call the Three Levels of Understanding.

First, I read through it once, twice, or however many times I need to in order to fully understand what the poem is saying on the most literal level. Forget about meaning or anything deeper than that. Just, what is the story of this poem? Let's practice with the previous poem, *Bird*.

Bird was actually based on a real-life event that happened to me. When I was about ten years old, a bird flew into our living room window and I found it injured on the ground outside. I felt so sorry for it! Luckily, my parents let me take it inside where we all took care of it for about a week until it felt better and was able to fly again. As much as I wanted to keep my new friend, I knew the right thing was to let it go. It probably had its own family that missed her.

I wrote *Bird* five years later when I was 15 years old. One of my favorite teachers ever, Dr. Levy, read it out loud to the class and talked about how rare it was to tell the story of a whole relationship in a short poem. Coming from him, this was a big deal, because this teacher had been close friends with T.S. Eliot, who is considered one of the greatest poets in history. I had no idea he would even think it was good, but it sparked my interest in really understanding poetry further.

Level 1. This is where we decipher the story of the poem. What happens?

In *Bird*, the story is that someone finds a wounded bird, nurses it back to health, and after letting it go, hopes that it will come back to visit. Pretty simple to understand even after the first read, but sometimes it can be much more complicated and take several readings, breaking down each line, or even doing outside research just to get through this step.

Level 2. Now that we understand the literal meaning, it's time to start thinking about what the poem is saying about the world.

Do you think most people would care for the bird? Why or why not?
Why do you think this person ended up caring for the bird?
Was it the right decision to let the bird go?
What could the bird represent?

Can you think of any situations where an accident happens and two different kinds of people or cultures ended up forming an unlikely bond? What kinds of people in the world could be similar to that wounded bird who needed help in order to survive?

These are all examples of taking the events of the poem and digging deeper to uncover what the poet might be trying to say about and the world and our existence.

Level 3. What does the poem say about yourself?

Would you care for the bird if it hit your window? Why or why not?
What if you were the bird? Have you ever been in a situation where something bad happened and your life was in the hands of someone you didn't know very well or at all?

Have you ever gotten hurt by something and were confused as to how and why it happened? Do you think the bird will come back and visit? How would you feel if it didn't?

The subject of this poem may not be one that resonates with you, and that's okay, too.

Hopefully you will find a poem in this book that speaks to you on a personal level.

My favorite poems are the ones where I feel like the poet was somehow writing about me, or at least had experienced what I had gone through.

You can sometimes get clues as to what the poet was trying to say by studying their lives and learning about what they believed in or what mattered to them the most. Most poets prefer not talk much about their poems' meanings because they want each reader to have their own reaction to it without any outside influence.

Just like your favorite foods, your favorite music, or your favorite color, there are no right or wrong answers when it comes to deciding what your favorite poems are. Don't listen to anyone who tells you the poem you like isn't as good as the one they like. It can be interesting to hear why they prefer one poem over another, but in the end, it's only people's opinions.

The poems that speak to you are like friends you can have in your head for the rest of your life—that you can think about and recite to yourself whenever you need them.

Do you think there might be a Level 4 level of understanding? Some people say there is, but that it's almost indescribable, like a secret level! I feel like I might have reached that level on just two poems I've read that are my absolute favorites.

Maybe you can reach Level 4 and tell me what it's like!

Wonderfully Weird

My body is going through changes.
That's normal, but mine seem the strangest.
I grew one giant ear
And my eyelids turned clear
And I think I have extra phalanges.

My knees became gnarled and knotty.
My face became dimpled and dotty.
I asked my mom why
Did I sprout a third eye?
She said, "Soon you'll grow into your body."

But nothing could stop me from growing.
And mutations showed no sign of slowing.
I asked my dad, "Pop,
Will this stuff ever stop?"
He said, "Never, now get back to mowing."

But it turned out my parents were right.
My body fit well overnight.
I am what I am,
But I sure ain't no sham.
I'm a wonderfully weird-looking sight!

I Do Not Want to Take a Bath

I do not want to take a bath
Said Bobby Buford Bean.
I'd rather do my chores or math
Than scrub my body clean.

I'd rather walk on rusty nails
Or paint my toenails green.
I'd rather eat a plate of snails.
Or sit out Halloween!

I'd rather stack up bales of hay.
I'd rather learn to type.
I'd rather put my toys away
Or clean the gutter pipe!

"I can't believe they called my bluff,"
Said Bobby, smelling ripe.
"This gutter cleaning's really tough.
Next time I'll hold my gripe."

Pancakes and Waffles

My mom's favorite breakfast
Is pancakes and waffles.
My mom says she loves them
But I say they're awful!

The butter is melty.
The syrup is sticky.
My mom says, "Just eat them."
But I think they're icky!

My dad's favorite breakfast
Is pancakes and waffles.
My dad says, "They're awesome!"
But I think they're awful!

The waffles are chewy
The pancakes are gooey.
My dad says, "So yummy!"
But I reply, "Phooey!"

My brother and sister
Love pancakes and waffles.
They tell me I'm crazy,
But I think they're awful!

Then one day they finally
Heard what I said.
On my plate was just toast
And a hardboiled egg.

I looked at my family,
Who each had a mouthful
Of buttery, melty
Gooey and chewy,
Sticky and crispy
Steamy and sweety…

Oh, what I'd give for a
Pancake or waffle.

Opossum

The first time I saw some opossum,
I prayed never again would I cross 'em.

Their tails were as pointy as rats'
And their eyes were like scarier cats.

Their snouts and their teeth were infernal.
Thank heavens they saunter nocturnal.

That's all that I thought and I knew…
Til I learned what they actually do.

While we're tacitly taking our rests,
They're happily out hunting pests.

On their backs they can carry their babies.
But they don't carry dangerous rabies.

"They're the only marsupial creature
That's outside Australia," said teacher.

Our towns would be dreadful without them.
I'm so glad that I learned all about them.

So if someone says, "Yikes! There's Opposum!"
Say, "Yay!" Cause opossums are awesome.

Finding Inspiration in Your Own Family

This next poem is the only one in the book that I did not write myself. It was actually written by my grandfather, Robert Taylor (see above photo).

It was a poem he had written for a creative writing class he took in college when he must have been just 19 or 20 years old. His very hard-to-please professor gave him an A grade for it, which may have been his proudest moment because he told me about it many times growing up, and he loved reciting the poem to me or anyone who would listen. He had it memorized and could break it out without a moment's thought or hesitation well into his 80s.

Grandpa Bob, as we called him, had dreams of becoming a writer and would often tell me about new novels he was working on, but I don't think he ever finished one. He put aside his writing dreams when he was young and ended up becoming a highly regarded psychologist and creator of psychological tests that are still used to this day.

Sadly, my grandfather did not live long enough to see my first book published, but I have always felt that I must have gotten my love for writing and poetry from him. This wonderful poem you are about to read may seem a bit silly at first, but every time I read it, I seem to find deeper hidden meanings and feel closer to understanding who my Grandpa Bob really was.

Minuet on a Z String
by Robert Taylor

Oh the geographic ballads are extensive.
And the singers sort of roam around the map.
With a girl in Mandalay, Mozambique, Paraguay,
Honolulu, Xanadu, or Yap.

Yes, it's hard to find a place we haven't mentioned,
Whether Russian, Swedish, Mexican, or Greek.
But my study of my chart until I know it all by heart
I believe I found a subject that's unique.

And I'll willingly explain
In the following refrain:

Oh I'll zigzag back to Zagazig and you,
Where the zephyrs in the zenith softly coo.
You'll be waiting my Suzanna in a Zagazig zenana
Feeding zulac to the Zebras in the zoo.

Yes, I'll soon be zooming thither while my heart beats in a dither
In my zeal I'll steal a zeppelin or two.
For the zinnias are growing and the zodiac is glowing
And my zest for Zagazig is ever new.
And I swear by Zoroaster that my heart is beating faster
As I zigzag back to Zagazig and you.

Should All Poems be Funny?
Not at all!

Poems can be about whatever you want. They can be sad, angry, happy, thought-provoking, or nothing at all. In fact, I think I've written a lot more serious poems than funny poems. Writing poetry helped me get through the hardest times in my life because I had a way to share my feelings, but I also didn't have to share my poems with anybody if I didn't want to.

I'm not sure if those poems will ever be published. If they aren't, it's no big deal because I wrote them for me. They comforted me when I felt lonely, shy, or depressed.

People weren't always there for me, but poetry – just a pen and some paper – always was.

This next poem and some others you'll find in this book aren't designed to make you laugh (even if they do). It's to help you feel better when you're going through a difficult or scary situation.

If your poetry is coming from a place of being true to yourself and genuine with your thoughts and feelings, that's all that really matters.

Pandemic

I'm afraid this pandemic is not very fun.
I'm missing my friends and I'm missing the sun.
I'm missing my coach and I'm missing my class
And I'm missing the breeze and the feel of soft grass.
I'm missing my sports teams and sitting in bleachers.
I'll tell you a secret — I'm missing my teachers.
I miss going to movies and watching parades
And parties and skating with shiny new blades.

On the other hand…

I like spending time with my mom and my cat
And talking with friends over video chat.
My sister is weird, but I'm glad that she's here.
We could dance and play games every day of the year.
I've learned all the states from New York to Virginia.
When I wear masks outside, I pretend I'm a ninja!
I've learned to bake cake and I've learned how to fry,
And there's 50 more things that I can't wait to try.

On the other hand…

I'm afraid this pandemic is not very fun.
 When it's over I can't wait to go out and run.
But I'm lucky my family is safe for today,
And I'll do what I need to to keep it that way.

I Married a Mermaid!

In case you haven't met my wife, beloved children's author Sheri Fink, well, I should tell you that I'm married to a mermaid. Just check out her website (SheriFink.com) and you can see real photos of her…fish tail and everything!

Sheri is the most magical and beautiful person I have ever met and I love writing poems that are inspired by her. While it's awesome being married to a mermaid, for this next poem I thought about what it might be like if someone really didn't like mermaids. Oh, the humanity!

Mermaids

My friends think that mermaids are totally cool,
But to me, they seem totally loony.
Wouldn't their eyes sting without any goggles?
And wouldn't their fingers get pruny?

Wouldn't their hair be a nightmare to comb?
And wouldn't their eardrums feel wooshy?
Wouldn't their food taste a tad bit too salty?
And how could they eat all that sushi?

Wouldn't the water be freezing in winter?
And wouldn't they tire of swishing?
Wouldn't sharks chase them all over the ocean
And don't get me started on fishing!

Some wish to be mermaids, and that is just fine.
But me? I am happy on land.
Feel free to grow fins and go live out your dream,
But I'll keep my bed free from all sand.

Penguins

The penguin braves both sleet and storm
To guard its eggs and keep them warm.
When penguins make their pick to mate,
They date, and then they incubate.

When penguins bond as man and wife,
They never part and mate for life.
Despite no wedding, I think it's neat-o
They always wear their best tuxedo.

Some Cool Poetry Facts

Sometimes poems can help you learn about a subject or help you remember complicated information.

Hundreds and even thousands of years ago, there were, of course, no electronics, and even books and paper could be hard to come by. So, people used songs and rhymes as a means of storing vast amounts of data and knowledge before there were hard drives. Why? Because rhyme and melody sticks easier in the brain than plain old facts. For your next test in school, try making up rhymes to remember important dates in history or biographical information.

Here's an example:

Theodore Roosevelt, he was no bore
Hunted for lions and fierce wild boar.
Made meat safe to eat and kept Cuba in line.
President from 1901 to '09.
Plus his face was carved high on Rushmore!

No need to worry much about meter when it's just for studying purposes.

I like to continue the tradition of educational poetry by writing poems about science, history, math and other subjects. In fact, I wrote a whole rhyming book called *Simon and the Solar System* about the planets in our solar system as extra credit for an astronomy class in college. A few kids have read that book and asked me why the moon wasn't in it. I tell them that I had to focus on the planets in that book, but I didn't want all the moon-lovers to feel left out, so this one's for you.

The Moon

The moon used to be part of Earth.
Then a meteor struck it near birth.
Rocks flew into space at high speed,
Then joined due to gravity's greed.
At first they looked ravaged and torn,
Then the moon and a new Earth were born.
They orbit, but never collide,
Bringing light during night and the tide.
And if meteors ever attack,
The moon, like a shield, has our back.

Can a Poem be Scary?

Yes, I love scary poems! They are especially fun to read aloud on Halloween or around a campfire at night.

You may remember me saying that one of my favorite poets was Edgar Allan Poe. He is the most famous writer of scary poems. You might know him as the author of *The Raven*, in which an unrelenting raven flies into a man's house and shrieks, "Nevermore!"

Here are three scary poems that I wrote, so if you get scared easily, you might want to skip them.

Do you like scary poems, scary books or scary movies? If so, you might be really good at writing a scary poem. Try writing one that's even scarier than these!

My Favorite Author

Yes, I have a favorite author
With whom I'd like to dine.
The problem is I'm rather scared
The meal would not go fine.

To write the things he writes about
His brain must need a sign.
Horrific things must happen
To inspire every line.

The forks and knives could come to life
The moment I recline.
They'd chase me 'round the dining room
And cut me like a vine!

There's a chance the friendly waiter,
Could have poisoned all the wine.
The chef may try to strangle me
With hidden butcher twine.

The soup could try to melt my tongue.
The bread has ill design.
The pickles may choose to revolt
And drown me in the brine.

If I am slayed in this café,
The fault would be all mine.
I dare not touch my pork chop—
T'would be Vengeance of the Swine!

How I wish my favorite author
Didn't tingle-fy my spine.
But sadly I must face my fears
When I dine with R.L. Stine.

The Creature in the Cave

There's a creature that dwells in a faraway cave
And it lurks in its lair that is also a grave
For the countless brave souls who have dared to confront it,
And many brave souls have endeavored to hunt it,
But found themselves wrapped…in the cold arms of death
As muscles of iron constricted their breath.

No one who's seen it has come back alive.
All that we know has been heard from their cries.
This is its name, but don't say it, just read it:
It's [Lupzom Karava]; this rule must be heeded,
For [Lupzom Karava] hears all that is said
And the sound of its name makes it rise from its bed!

Oh no! Whoever who just said it will surely be dead.

It howls as the sound waves ske-dank down its spine
And its teeth start to tingle and salivate slime.
It's eyes, red and wide, glow like sparks in the dark!
And the spikes on its back spring up ready and sharp.
As it raises its talons and razor-edged tail,
The hunt for its victim begins without fail.

It flies through the starlight in frightening silence
To make this soul pay for its daring defiance.
It follows the breath that it smelled in its name
And it flies to the window and eyes its fresh game.

It suddenly snarls! The window glass shatters!
The heart of its victim ga-thumps as it patters!
It crawls in the room and it drools on the floor.
It smashes the furniture, screeches, and roars!

The victim shouts helplessly [Lupzom Karava!],
Which makes its blood boil and poor out like lava!

It gruesomely inches, the victim is sweating,
Then [Lupzom Karava!] he shouts while he's wetting

His pants, for he knows that his life will be ending,
But what now is happening? The beast is descending
In spasms and sobbing with horrible shame!
Something has hurt it! The sound of its name!

It spits and it thrashes with desperate violence,
But even this outburst cannot create silence,
For its name is proclaimed now again and again!
And it can't kill the truth so it flees to its den.

It is safe in its lair, it is safe as a myth.
But to be all forgotten, now that would be bliss.
So it rests in its cave and repairs all its wounds.
It knows it shall see yet a million more moons.

Defeat is a setback but not a big deal.
It will live until everyone knows that it's real.

Beware!

Beware beware
Oh little child!
Beware the monsters and the trolls!
Beware the webs
And viruses
That pop out from the scrolls.

Beware Beware
Oh little one!
Beware the ads and traps they set!
Beware the clicks
To darkest paths
When wandering the internet!

What is Wordplay?

Sometimes I like to write poems for no other reason other than I want to have fun with words. That's what wordplay is! Just playing around with words and language.

The English language is amazing for wordplay because it's a mixture of so many different languages, with so many crazy rules, exceptions, pronunciations, and contradictions.

That fact that English is a complete mess is actually what makes it so much fun to play with.

Examples of wordplay can be alliteration, where you have the same consonant sound over and over, such as: Derek danced dynamically in Denmark.

There's also assonance, where you have the repetition of vowel sounds, such as: Mick the pig is incredibly itchy.

I also like to deconstruct words to make new words and try to fit it into a poem, such as:

I couldn't tell if
The stiff,
Furry caterpillar
Looked more like cat or pillar.

Just sitting down and having fun with words is a great way to forget about the 'seriousness' of poetry and all the deeper meanings and just hone your skills with using words in new, creative ways.

Here are some poems, which I can assure you, have absolutely no meaning. They're just me having fun with words.

The poem on the next page is not technically a poem, though it has poetic elements to it. Try reading some of these sentences to friends or family and see if they can understand you!

I is Funny

I is a funny sound because it can be so many things.

For instance, "I" can be used to indicate myself, but the same sound is also an eye.

BUT, not only can it be an eye, you can also "eye" something if you see it.

So… if I see an eye, I eye an eye.

BUT, here's where things start to get tricky. I'm in the army and when we need to confirm that we received an order, we say, "aye-aye!" which is pronounced eye-eye.

So… if I see someone aye-aye, I eye an aye-aye.

BUT, here's where things get really tricky.

My captain in the army is named Captain Ai, which is pronounced Captain 'Eye,' but we just call him Ai for short.

So… whenever I see Captain Ai give an aye-aye… I eye Ai aye-aye.

BUT, here's where things get WEIRD.

When your superior officer gives you an aye-aye, it's expected that you give an aye-aye back.

So… If I eye Ai aye-aye, I aye-aye Ai.

BUT, here's where things get REALLY weird.

Captain Ai has a bionic eye that has a mind of its own. He isn't super creative and named his bionic eye, Eye.

So… when Eye pops out of Ai's head and falls onto the ground while Ai is giving an aye-aye… I eye Eye eye Ai aye-aye and I aye-aye Ai.

BUT, here's where things get CRAZY.

Eye is programmed to say aye-aye when it pops out of Captain Ai so that Ai will be able to locate it on the ground. When Eye says aye-aye, it's expected that I and any other soldier, including Captain Ai, say aye-aye back.

So, when I eye Eye aye-aye Ai, I eye Ai aye-aye Eye. Then I aye-aye Eye, I aye-aye Ai, and I eye Eye aye-aye I.

BUT, here's where things get REALLY crazy.

There's a kind of nocturnal lemur from Madagascar called an aye-aye. It's true. Captain Ai went on a mission to Madagascar and brought one back to the base as his pet and, of course, named it Aye-Aye. Unfortunately, Ai taught Aye-Aye to aye-aye.

So, when I eye Aye-Aye aye-aye Ai, I aye-aye Aye-Aye, I aye-aye Ai, I aye-aye Eye, I eye Eye aye-aye Aye-Aye, I eye Eye aye-aye Ai, I eye Aye-Aye aye-aye Eye, I eye Aye-Aye aye-aye Ai, I eye Ai aye-aye Aye-Aye, I eye Ai aye-aye Eye, and I eye Eye aye-aye Ai.

Then, Ai, Eye, Aye-Aye, and I eye every single soldier on the base aye-aye Aye-Aye, Eye, Ai, and I.

Goodbye.

The Gnu I Knew

One day I went to the zoo.

When I met a gnu at the zoo,
I knew a gnu.

When she showed me papers proving she was a gnu,
I knew I knew a gnu.

When the gnu told me she had a big announcement,
I knew a gnu with news.

When the gnu invited me to come meet her new baby,
I knew a gnu and a new gnu.

When I learned the new gnu was born at 12:00 pm,
I knew a gnu and a new noon gnu.

When I found out the baby gnu had a twin,
I knew a gnu and two new noon gnus.

When we all decided to travel down the river together,
I canoed with the gnu I knew and two new noon gnus.

When the canoe went over a waterfall and crashed through a Beaver family's chimney,
The canoe with the gnu I knew and two new noon gnus flew through a flue.

When the canoe landed on a toy train set and got eaten by the family of beavers,
The canoe with the gnu I knew and two new noon gnus that flew through the flue got chewed on a choo-choo!

The gnu I knew and her two new noon gnus were a very gloomy crew.
The canoe had been chewed to the screws and the two new noon gnus had blue bruises too!

There wasn't anything else we could do,
So we went back to the zoo.

When I waved goodbye to the gnu, I said,
Too-ta-loo, Gnu!

Then, a little girl asked me, "Who's your friend?"

I said, "That is a gnu."

She said, "That's not a gnu! That's a ewe!"

I said to the gnu, "Wait a second, are you a ewe?"

"I have no clue," said the gnu, who was possibly a ewe. "Do you?"

I thought the gnu was a gnu, but now I had no clue what was true.

Maybe it was half ewe, half gnu. If only ewe-gnu.

Bird Ranks

Hummingbirds are stunning birds.
I like them more than running birds
Like roadrunners and ostriches,
But not mockingbirds nor partridges.

Myna birds are finer birds,
But they are not my kinda birds.
If ever I were buyin' a bird,
I'd try and find a tinier bird.

What is the Purpose of Poetry?

Many years ago, before the advent of movies, TV, videogames and digital music, painters and poets were the rock stars of their age.

Famous poets could fill entire arenas with their readings and a spectacular new painting could make front-page news.

Times have certainly changed and making a living as a full-time poet is far more difficult than it used to be, but the important role of poetry in our world is still alive and strong.

Slam poets perform for massive audiences and spoken word shows are tremendously popular and boast ravenous fans for the best wordsmiths. Battle rappers play for rowdy crowds trying to outwit one another in verbal rhyming duels. Many choose to turn poetry into music like many of today's rappers and hip-hop artists. Writers like Dr. Seuss can turn poetry into classic stories that parents read to their children every night.

Poetry is with us and around us every day. Over time it just evolves and takes on new forms.

But what is the purpose of it all? I suppose that varies from poet to poet. Some are relentlessly seeking beauty and truth. Some may just want to entertain people. Some may only want to write a poem as a gift to someone that will make that person feel special.

Poetry's main purpose for me has always been to help me get through difficult times. When I felt angry or hurt, I would try and create something good and beautiful so that at least the pain had a purpose. When my parents divorced, I would write about how my life was actually nothing like I thought it was. On the days after the terrorist attack on 9/11, I would write about how sad I felt, and how I saw the world changing and wondered what it would become. When I felt heartbroken, I would write poems questioning if I would ever find true love. (Luckily I did!)

When I was in a funny mood, I wrote poems that I hoped would make people, and especially children, laugh like crazy. Do you think poetry is important? Is it as important as math and science? These are very big questions that your generation is going to have to grapple with.

Tightrope

The rope extends out sensitively.
We venture outward tentatively.
Balancing one foot in front of the other.
Hoping for one fate, dreading another.
The pace is determined, worries diminish.
The crowd urges on, demanding we finish.
But we're less than halfway across!
Nervously twitching, like gelatin sauce.
A faulty string will make us fall.
Caution returns. We continue to crawl…

Was it worth it to walk on the tightrope?

The Dragon and the Fly

The most fearsome creature that I ever knew
Was a dragon afraid of the fire it blew.
He'd shudder aghast at the tiniest spark,
So his food remained cold and his cave remained dark.

At every new land, mobs arrived at his porch,
Then he'd fly away fast at the light of one torch.
There was no place to rest, nor a home of his own.
There was no place to fly where he hadn't yet flown.

On the loneliest mountain, unclimb-ably high,
Was the last place he found…where he thought he would die.

Then one day a horsefly crawled onto his nose.
They stared at each other, not shifting their pose.
The dragon said, "Leave! Are you not scared to die?"
The fly said, "I would, but I'm too scared to fly."

The dragon laughed, "Ha! Flying's what a fly does!
It's right in your name, so please fly off now, buzz!"
But the fly didn't move. It just trembled with fear.
"If I move I may fall, so I think I'll stay here."

It stayed there for hours, then days turned to weeks.
Drinking tears that rolled down from the sad dragon's cheeks.

The fly became stronger, but still never flew.
Til one day the dragon knew just what to do.
It lit a small flame from the end of its nose,
And the heat began burning the fly's little toes.

The dragon was shaking, but the flame wasn't fleeting,
And soon the fly's wings began busily beating.
Like a rocket the fly quickly zipped through the light.
Its head got some bumps, but it flew through the night.

The dragon stopped shaking. The flicker remained.
He opened his jaws feeling free and unchained.

He crawled from his cave… saw the world far below.
With a geyser of fire, he shouted, "Let's go!"

Caterpillar

The caterpillar makes a journey
Up to places soft and ferny.
Dangling from a twig or leaf,
Its larval stage is far too brief,
For once a moth, it somehow knows
To make a beeline for my clothes.

Learning from Other Writers

When you're starting to write your own poems, it can be fun to try and mimic other poets in order to get the hang of it. Great comedians begin by doing the routines of their favorite comedians for their friends and family. Great artists will draw or paint in the style of their favorite artists before creating their own style.

This poem is kind of like that. It's an homage to my biggest inspiration for this book, Shel Silverstein. In his classic book of poems *Where the Sidewalk Ends*, Shel Silverstein wrote a poem called Jimmy Jet and his TV Set. I read that one recently and wondered how he might have written that poem today with all the new technology kids are into. Here's what I thought he might have written.

Jimmy Joe James and his Videogames

There once was a child
Named Jimmy Joe James
Who couldn't stop playing
His videogames.

He played on his X-box
He played on his Switch,
Then switched to his Sony
Without any glitch.

He played at the table
He played during class.
In soccer he played
While he ran through the grass.

He played while he prayed
And he prayed while he played.
He played in his sleep
And he played on parade.

When friends would stop by
There was no interacting.
He told them to leave because
Friends were distracting.

He no longer walked
So they pushed him in strollers.
Til one day his hands became
Double controllers.

His nails became buttons
His eyes became screens.
His ears picked up wi-fi
From all the machines.

Jimmy Joe had transformed
To a living game system!
His friends came to visit
And no longer missed him.

They call him the Game-Boy —
Half-boy and half-game.
Kids love to play Jimmy,
At least… what he became.

The Fudge Defense

I stood before the judge,
My heart awash with worry.
"I did not eat the fudge!"
I cried out to the jury.

"There's chocolate on your face,"
Replied the doubtful judge.
I said, "Please hear my case.
I say it's just a smudge."

The judge said, "Very well,
The defendant may proceed."
I said, "The fudge ball simply fell,
I cleaned it with great speed!"

I looked across the courtroom.
The jury was still out.
I looked up at the judge,
Who clearly still had doubt.

The judge inhaled my breath.
"That's fudge," she sternly said.
She sentenced me to death.
No games, just straight to bed.

I said, "The judge is wrong!
Can the jury find another?"
The jury said, "Roberto,
Just listen to your mother."

What's the Difference Between Song Lyrics and Poetry?

It's kind of strange when you think about it, but almost every song has a rhythm and rhyme scheme just like poetry. I remember when I was a child asking my parents and teachers why songs rhymed. All they could tell me was, "Because it makes them sound better."

I didn't get into playing music until I was in college. I loved writing silly songs along with my silly poems throughout childhood, but I didn't know how to play an instrument well enough to actually make them sound like a real song. So, I taught myself how to play a guitar and now I've produced dozens of songs and a whole musical called King Kalimari. It's about a young wizard's apprentice who must stop an army of squids from attacking the kingdom. Yeah, it's weird.

Song lyrics are often indistinguishable from poetry and the best song lyrics usually can stand on their own as great poems. Songs have their own forms, though, where there is a "chorus" or "hook" that repeats after the verses, so there is a lot more repetition than you would find in most poems.

Ultimately the purpose of the song lyrics is to be in service of the melody and tone of a song. Therefore, great song lyrics will oftentimes look like a simple or nonsensical poem on paper, but when set to music, everything makes sense and they work perfectly. Folk singer Bob Dylan is often considered one of the greatest poets and song lyricists of all time, so much so that he was awarded the Nobel Prize for Literature in 2016. Can you think of any other great lyricists whose lyrics are also great poetry?

Below is a song from King Kalimari that I think holds up pretty well as a poem. During the repeating chorus there's a certain sound that hits on the same beat every time. Can you tell what it is?

If you'd like to hear what the song sounds like, you can go to DerekTaylorKent.com/HystericalRhymes and hear it for free sung by the original actors from the show.

Ahoy We Go! (song)

Ahoy we go, a-sailing you know,
A-fishin' around the bay.
Efficiently fishin' for fish and we're wishin'
For fish so we're fishin' today!

And when we catch the fish
We're gonna drag 'em upon the boat.
We'll cut 'em and gut 'em and sell 'em for somethin'
And that'll be all she wrote!

Ahoy we go, a-sailing you know,
A-fishin' around the bay.
Efficiently fishin' for fish and we're wishin'
For fish so we're fishin' today!

Oh, we sailed the sea all mornin'
And our nets are filled with fish!
So you can have a carcass with
Some garnish on your dish!

Ahoy we go, a-sailing you know,
A-fishin' around the bay.
Efficiently fishin' for fish and we're wishin'
For fish so we're fishin' today!

Oh, the mighty ship is loaded
And the crew is loaded too.
We'll hoist up loads of mackerels
And salmon and tuna too!

Ahoy we go, a-sailing you know,
A-fishin' around the bay.
Sufficiently fishin' for fish and we're wishin'
For fish so we're fishin' today.
Proficiently fishin' for fish and we're wishin'
For fish so we're fishin' today!

Ahoy!

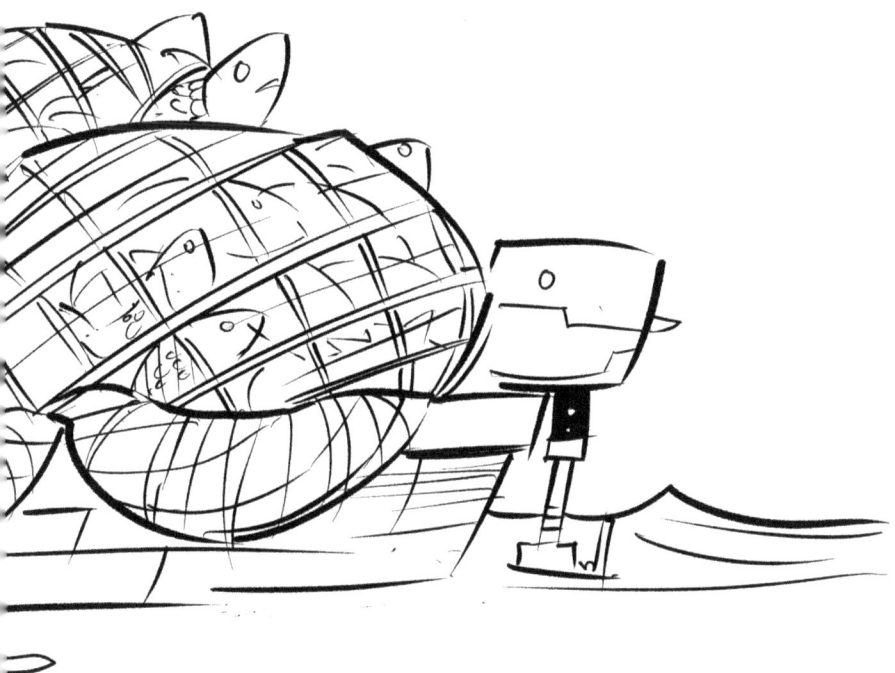

A Poetic Form as Easy as 1-2-3

An ABC poem is a specific type of poem where each word in the poem starts with the next letter in the alphabet. I first heard about this kind of poem when I discovered one written by one of my favorite poets, Robert Pinsky. It's simply called ABC and I encourage all of you to look it up.

Below are a few of my attempts at this form. Please note that 'X-Chromosome' means a girl in the first poem, which you'll learn about in science class one day.

ABCs

Are boys creepy?
Don't ever forget
Girls hide insects.
Jars keep little
Millipedes, nightcrawlers
Or predatory quick
Ravenous spiders
Trapping unsuspecting
Victim weevils.
X-chromosomes yell,
Zoinks!

A brilliant conductor directed euphoric fantasias.
Grateful hordes imbibe
Joyful keys,
Lifting Mozart.
New orchestral percussion quartets
Reimagine symphonies.
Tambourines, ukuleles, violins, woodwinds, xylophones
Yield zealotry.

Apparently bears can dance.
Extra fancy grizzlies hibernate in jumpsuits.
Kodiaks learn moves nightly.
Obsessed pandas
Quietly re-emerge
Seeking Tango umpires,
Victorious waltz X-hibitions,
yelping zookeepers.

Brushing your Teeth

Brushing your teeth is extremely important,
But not as important as scrubbing your feet.
The reason is feet are extremely absorbent
And pick up the filth that ends up on the street.

Scrubbing your feet is extremely important,
But not as important as washing your sheets.
The reason is sheets soak up sweat while you're dormant,
Which make them more sticky than syrupy sweets!

Washing your sheets is extremely important,
But not as important as brushing your teeth.
The reason is teeth can become quite abhorrent
When bits of old meat stick between and beneath.

Brushing your teeth is extremely important,
But not as important as wiping your butt.
The reason is, well, if I'm your informant,
You might have a problem, so keep your pants shut.

Shorts

I love to play sports
Of all kinds and all sorts
But I never get picked by a club or a team
And I think it's because of my shorts.

My shorts are not short.
They hang down to the court.
They're so long they've become their own meme.
And my classmates do nothing but snort.

Don't buy the reports
Of my callous cohorts
For my shorts are not pants like they seem.
To that I have valid retorts.

My legs are real short
And I've got a bad wart
So these shorts help me build self-esteem.
So pick me and let us cavort!

Math Tricks

I used to think that math was hard.
Each test I took, I blew it.
But then I learned some tips and tricks
That made it fun to do it!

When squaring things that end in 5.
Impress your friends with this cool trick,
Like 25 times 25 or 85 times 85.
Can you do it in a lick?

Here's the trick, remember this:
They always end in 25.
Try it on your calculator.
Take it for a drive.

Just multiply the digit
With the number next in line.
25 is 2 times 3
And 85 is 8 times 9.

25 times 25 is just 2 times 3 then 25.
85 times 85 is 8 times 9 then 25.
Do you have the answer yet?
It's almost hard to miss... 625 and 7225!
There's dozens more fun tricks like this.
Oh what numeric bliss!

Baseball Cap

When you play baseball
And everyday you wear the same cap,
The salt is left from your sweat
And forms a crusty, white helmet.

To clean the baseball cap,
You must put it in the dishwasher;
And that gets the job done.
It makes it smell really good too.

After my cap was cleaned,
I left it on the floor.
My cat smelled it from across the house,
Came into my room, and fell asleep inside it.

So, I had to leave my cap on the floor for her
Every day after school.
That's how she became the Cat in the Hat.

The above poem is another one that I wrote in high school and is a true story. It's also the closest I come to writing free verse in this book, which makes the end all the more funny to me.

The Alien

I used to be afraid of folks
With different looks or names.
I didn't want to make new friends
And wished we looked the same.

But then I met an alien
When walking through a wood.
It spoke to me in clicks and beeps
I strangely understood.

"My name is Glarp," the creature beeped,
"Come ride my ship with me?"
I thought and said, "Okay, why not?
My afternoon is free."

In moments we touched down upon
A planet filled with Glarps.
They looked like ferrets mixed with monkeys,
Manta rays and carps.

They pointed and they laughed at me.
"This one's the strangest yet!
How does it breathe? How does it speak?
It's barely even wet!"

"Can it see in all dimensions?
Is its brain a heap of gravel?
Does it even know the secret of
Galactic stellar travel?"

They pressed and they prodded my torso.
They pulled and they pinched at my face.
"Let's dissect it!" Glarp contended,
"Then dump it back out into space."

I didn't like this feeling
So I ran back to the ship.
I said, "Please take me back to Earth,"
And had an instant trip.

But back on Earth, ten years had passed,
Though I'd not aged a day.
I'm sure that Einstein could explain it
Easily away.

When I meet folks who are different,
Now I treat them like a star.
I learned we're all just aliens,
Depending where we are.

The Greatest Poem Ever Written?

This next poem I spent over twenty years toiling over night and day. It kept me up at nights in sleepless sweats trying to come up with the perfect wording for each prodigious line. I finally finished it and am able to sleep once again. It's so meaningful and important that an illustration would only diminish its impact and I have forbidden it. Is it the greatest poem ever written? Probably. But I'll let you be the judge.

My Thumb Hurts

My thumb hurts.
My thumb hurts.
And you know what?
My thumb hurts.

Purple Pimples

If you pop a normal pimple
You may end up with a dimple.
But if pimple turns to purple
Well, the plan is not that simple.

When a purple pimple tickles,
You can scratch it with a sickle.
You may think you found the trick
But then the itch will quickly trickle.

When the trickle starts to wiggle
You may have the need the giggle,
But the pimple will not giggle,
It will double and then triple!

Soon the single purple pimple
Will be millions, any wimp'll
Have no choice but simply grumble
Being purple, feeling crippled.

So don't pop a purple pimple.
Don't you scratch a purple pimple.
Don't you touch a purple pimple.
Don't you patch a purple pimple.

On the subject of these pimples
You have taken quite an earful.
But the truth is they are fiction,
So relax and don't be fearful.

The Whimsical Worm

Ever witnessed or wondered what lies below ground?
Yes, there's mud, dirt, and muck, I can fully affirm.
But there's also a fellow I'm glad to have found.
He's Wendell J. Wiggle – the whimsical worm!

When you think of a worm, there's not much to be thought.
They slither through soil and munch upon mulch.
They wriggle in tunnels and revel in rot,
And most commonly dwell in a garden or gulch.

Of sparkles and rainbows and daring to dream,
No worm ever cared since worm records were kept.
But Wendell learned much from our days by the stream,
And a life without whimsy was why Wendell wept.

I remember the day Wendell popped out his head.
I was writing a story of mermaids below.
He asked me, 'What are those?" and after I said,
He asked me to share with him all that I know.

So I told him of unicorns prancing through fields.
I told him of rocket ships blasting through space.
I told him of dragons and knights with their shields.
Wendell wanted to wander in such a wide place.

He asked me to take him to faraway lands.
I told him that sadly those places aren't real.
They're only in books that we hold in our hands,
But they live in our hearts through the dreams that we feel.

Each day I met Wendell, he inched up my arm.
He soaked up each story from dusk until dawn.
For months he just listened and hung like a charm,
Til one day I looked and saw Wendell was gone.

Perhaps I said something that scared him away.
Perhaps he was spotted and eaten by birds.
All of these thoughts made my mornings so grey,
I imagined him lost in an ocean of words.

But month after month I returned to our spot.
I read books aloud in the hopes he would hear.
But the rocks didn't laugh and the river cared not,
Then one day I saw something awfully queer.

The dimmest of lights glowed from under a stone.
I rolled the stone over and peered deep within.
A child-sized tunnel that twinkled and shone,
Tempted me forward and beckoned me in.

I wriggled and twisted and squeezed my way through,
Til I dropped in a cavern and opened my eyes.
A whimsical wonderland blazed into view,
And Wendell J. Wiggle flew down from the skies.

Yes, Wendell the worm now had butterfly wings,
A unicorn horn and a bright mermaid tail.
I still have no clue how he made all those things,
As he fluttered before me and said, "Let's set sail!"

Then glowworms ignited like millions of stars!
Fireflies formed in the shape of a ship!
A rocket took off on a mission to Mars
And the pond rippled rainbows with each glowing drip.

Then Wendell dropped down, glowing bright as a lantern.
He said, "I am sorry for taking so long.
I worked night and day to create you this cavern.
Now you'll always have someplace you know you belong."

So when speaking to worms, there is no need to taunt it.
There's no need to smush it or say 'eww' or squirm.
Wendell taught me the world can be just how you want it.
I'll never forget him – the Whimsical Worm.

50 Laugh-Out-Loud Limericks
part 2

What is a Limerick?

I know I said before that I love poetry, but of all the different poetic forms, limericks are my favorite. I was introduced to the limerick poetry form by a high school teacher named Mr. Azhar.

Limericks have a set pattern of AABBA and traditionally have a specific meter. Here's a limerick I wrote about limericks.

A limerick has meter and time,
And the second line follows in rhyme.
The third line's absurd
The fourth rhymes with the third
And the fifth line is always the punch line.

Why do I love limericks so much? I guess it's because I love humor, and a limerick has the same structure of a joke. It starts with a set up. The first two lines establish the premise and rhyme with each other.

The second two lines take the set up and explore it. They rhyme with each other and are shorter lines.

The fifth and final line rhymes with the first two lines, and offers a clever twist, a profound idea, or climax of wordplay that should feel like a perfect end to a joke or a satisfying conclusion to the set up.

What really got me obsessed with limericks was a particular limerick I read in a poetry class in high school. It went like this:

A tutor who tooted the flute
Tried to teach two young tooters to toot.
Said the two to the tutor,
"Is it harder to toot or
To tutor two tooters to toot?"

To me, that's a perfect limerick and amazing wordplay. The author found a clever nuance in the English language and exploited it to its maximum potential and was also able to tell a funny story with it. That led me on my quest to find other "loopholes" in the English language and expose them through limerick.

Did I succeed? That will be for you to judge. But I hope you have as much fun reading them as I had writing them.

Golfin' Dolphin

It's tough to play golf with a dolphin.
They have no arms or legs – they are all fin.
What makes golfing fun
Is the rare hole-in-one,
And they have one! So take dolphin golfin'!

The Handy Kid

There once was a kid who was handy.
At house-building he was quite dandy.
He built our new wing
On his week off in spring
And the best part? We paid him with candy!

Spaghetti

In the era right after the Ice Age
Folks topped their spaghetti with sausage.
When pork was replaced
With tomato-based-paste
The first taste marked the start of the Sauce Age.

A Wiener and Sausage

A wiener and sausage were keener
To settle whose body was leaner.
When tallies came in
Wiener said with a grin,
 "I was destined to win - I'm a wiener!"

Sorry for PUN-ishing You!

One of the popular ways to find humor is to come up with creative puns. What is a pun? A pun is a joke that makes a play on words. A pun uses words that have more than one meaning, or words that sound similar but have different meanings, and the realization of that makes us laugh.

Here are a few famous puns:

I was struggling to figure out how lightning works, but then it struck me.
A chicken crossing the road is truly poultry in motion.
Reading while sunbathing makes you well red.
A hardboiled egg every morning is hard to beat.

Here are some of my favorites that you may remember from earlier in the book:

If only ewe-gnu.

The pun is on the common phrase, if only you knew.

"I was destined to win - I'm a wiener!"

Wiener sounds like winner.

Try re-reading the book and see if you can find all of the puns. There's a whole lot more coming up, and I bet you'll notice them.

Can you come up with your own puns? A fun way to practice is to think of titles from books, movies or TV and change the sounds of one of the words to make it sound like a totally different story.

For instance, Harry Plopper is the story of a magical pig. (That one is from The Simpsons)

Diary of a Shrimpy Squid is about a really small giant squid. (That one is mine)

A Bee

A bee had to sing ABC,
And she wanted an A, not a B.
After singing the D
She forgot to say E,
And when bee got an F, she said, "Gee!"

New Jersey

There once was a boy from New Jersey
Whose basketball team begged for mercy.
They purchased new shirts
And were winning in spurts!
So don't ever discount a new jersey.

The Best Pets

If you'd like to talk pets well then let's
Discuss features of all the best pets.
Some pets can be pests
And some pests can be pets
But the best pets ingest pests the best.

A Cattle Tale

Do NOT let your snakes near your cattle.
Cows get spooked by their hiss or their rattle.
But the hiss of your cat
Is a worse hiss than that,
So if snakes don't scare cattle, then cat'll.

To Bet in Tibet

Bates liked to bet in Tibet
But he also liked taking big bets.
Said Bates to a bettor:
Is it better to bet or
To bait a big better to bet?

Scott in Knots

I know of a very strange Scott
Who ties all his shoes in a knot.
And if you suppose
Why he doesn't tie bows
As opposed to those knots, well, why not?

Do I Need to Have Artwork to Go with My Poetry?

Well, that's totally up to you!

I love having artwork with my poetry because I think it can really add to the experience and turn a normal laugh into a big laugh.

Sometimes, though, you may want to inspire people to use their imaginations and create their own images in their heads without the influence of an artist's vision.

I am not a very good artist, so if I want to have artwork in my books, I ask a friend to do it or work with a professional artist. It can be really cool to see how different artists interpret your words and bring their own ideas to the illustrations.

If you can write and draw, then you are amazingly talented and could have a very successful career creating illustrated books.

And don't be fooled into thinking illustrated books are only for kids! Some of the greatest writers of all time like Robert Louis Stevenson and William Blake created beautifully illustrated books of poetry that were huge hits in their day. Today, graphic novels and comic books are booming in popularity as well, so that's another great medium where you can combine artwork and writing.

Would you have done a different drawing for any of the poems you read so far? Could you add something to them to make them even funnier?

I can't wait to see what you'd do!

Eating and Kneading

A kneader who liked to knead meat
Kneaded meat by the meter, not feet.
While many just meet her
It's neater to feed her
For eating while kneading's a feat!

Rabbit

If your dream is to capture a rabbit,
You must train every day like it's habit.
Practice leaping up knolls
And then diving through holes,
But the truth is, you'll still never nab it.

Bull Training

At bull-training Billy was able.
His student bulls slept in a stable.
But one starry night
Billy's students took flight,
Had he caught sight he might have yelled, "Stay, bull!"

Beaver

One day Betty walked by a beaver,
But her boyfriend just wouldn't believe her.
Without but a pout
She packed up and moved out
'Cause his doubt about beavers just peeved her.

Constrictor

If constricting were strictly restricted
A constrictor would feel quite conflicted.
If squeezing is cheating,
The law says no eating!
Good thing my snake can't be convicted.

Rapping Raptor

At rapping a raptor was apt.
His concerts kept every crowd rapt.
A pal asked him after
Would you like your meal wrapped or
Shall we lock down and keep the crowd trapped?

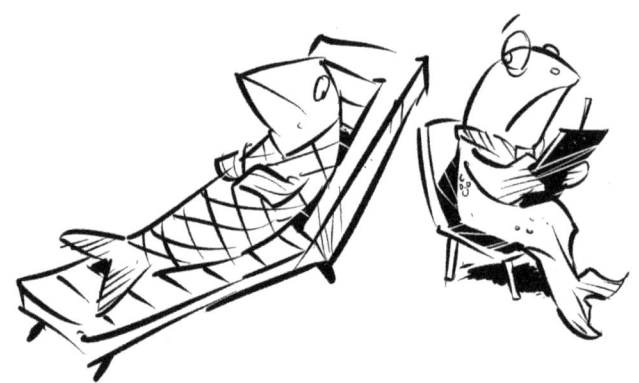

Snapper

If you happen to chat with a snapper
He may tell you his life's in the crapper.
Red snappers are blue
'Cause they hate their red hue,
But if they were blue, they'd be happier.

She Sells Shells

Nell liked to sell shells from her cellar,
Though the sales for her shells were not stellar.
Her feller said, "Nell,
On the shore they'd sell well,
But a cellar ain't swell for a seller."

Harry

Harry yearned for a Mary to marry,
But in Cary there's nary a Mary.
So he ferried to Leeds
Where there's Marys like weeds
Found a Mary to marry
And merrily carried his Mary to Cary.

(Sorry this one broke from form a bit, but I couldn't resist.)

Unicorn

A unicorn yearned for a horn
That wasn't so golden and shorn.
"What nobody knows
Is I'm hounded by crows
For what grows on my crown looks like corn!"

Smelly Celery

If your goal is to sell lots of celery,
You must tend to the smell necessarily.
Good celery sellers
Won't sell from their cellars
For cellars will make them smell cellary.

Train on a Plane

A trainer who trains on a plane,
Thinks that training on planes is a pain.
"If I could," said the trainer
"I'd train on a train or
On plains, but it's hard to ex-plane."

Sweater Weather

A sweater ought not wear a sweater,
For a sweater will make sweater wetter.
But if weather is wet
Sweater's better I bet.
Did the sweat make him wet or the weather?

Giraffes

Giraffes are as funny as heck.
But giraffes never laugh, you can check.
Don't fall for the rumor
Giraffes have no humor,
For laughs just get stuck in their neck!

Sheri the Mermaid

My wife is a mermaid named Sheri,
Though I feel like she might be a fairy.
'Cause she likes sparkly things
And takes pictures with wings
And thinks swimming in oceans is scary!

Bad Puppy

There's nothing as cute as a puppy.
Except when it makes indoor pup pee.
Before they are trained
They may wee unrestrained
But be patient and soon they'll grow uppy!

Toy in a Toilet

If your toy ever falls in the toilet,
You will probably break it or spoil it.
But if toy can be rushed-out
Without getting flushed out,
Before you enjoy it, just boil it.

Ben Franklin

Ben Franklin was quite the eccentric.
He contended that lightning's electric.
With a key and a kite
On a dark, stormy night
He was right! What an excellent trick!

Ferret or Parrot?

For my birthday I asked for a parrot.
But instead I received a new ferret.
My parents misheard
My request for a bird.
We'd return it, but cannot ensnare it!

Don't Buy a House from a Turkey

I once bought a house from a Turkey,
Though its talk of the home was quite murky.
Turkey said it was ready,
Yet it looked like a Yeti
Had lived there! T'was not at all turn-key.

Castles are a Hassle

I once dreamed of building a castle.
But now it just seems like a hassle.
With constant besieging
And high cost of heating
If invaders don't kill you, the gas'll.

Minnie

There once was a man from Minnesota,
Whose girlfriend, named Minnie, drank soda.
She drank the last drop
And his heart went ker-plop!
Cause he wanted to taste Minnie's soda.

Hungry Koala

When Koala ate dry eucalyptus,
His friend said, "Here's Ranch. You can dip this."
So Koala dipped leaf
And was in disbelief,
"You have made eucalyptus delicious!"

Dental Potential

Tooth-brushing is super essential,
Or your cavities could get torrential.
Don't brush with a paintbrush
Just brush with a toothbrush
To realize your dental potential.

Driving to Mars

They say Mars is too far for a car,
But I once drove my car to a star.
All right, it was Starbucks,
But I don't give two clucks,
All I need is the world's biggest pee jar.

Snickers

Somehow each time I eat Snickers
It elicits a series of snickers.
Is it the sounds that I make?
Does my upper lip quake?
It could not be these super-cool knickers.

Fancy Mosquito

There once was a fancy mosquito,
Who dressed up to dine in tuxedo.
"I'm the king of the night!"
He proclaims with each bite,
"So why would I dine incognito?"

Starfish

Starfish aren't nimble, but clever.
Seen one with no legs? I bet never.
Should there be an attack,
Any limb can grow back.
They just crack, "I'll be fine, it's a sever!"

Smelly Jelly

Good jelly is not ever smelly.
If it's smelly it may hurt your belly.
But if jelly smells great,
Dump the jar on my plate!
Mate, don't hate on my plate, you're just jeally!

When Fruit Goes Bad

After calls of a very strange robbery,
Detectives found seeds of a raw berry.
So they sounded alarms
That a berry grew arms,
And the manhunt began for armed strawberry.

The berry was caught on the lam,
And the judge had a very sick plan.
They sent him to prison
To work in the kitchen
Where his job was to cook all the jam!

Nintendo

It's fun to play games on Nintendo.
But alone the fun can't reach crescendo.
You may not get bored
With your console or board,
But it's best to play games with a friend, though.

Scuba with a Tuba

A horn-blower went to Aruba.
After concerts he liked to go scuba.
But his horn felt deprived,
So together they dived,
And a tuna got stuck in the tuba.

Bros and Bots

If there's one thing I hate it's a robot.
For Christmas it's what my big bro got.
He trained it in loogies
Plus wedgies and noogies.
Bros and bots should be nice, but they're so not.

Basketball is Weird

I just don't get the rulebook of basketball.
Until now I've been too scared to ask at all.
If no traveling's allowed
How do teams find a crowd?
Yes I do think these rules need an overhaul.

Glass Cows and Moss Cows

Moscow's mountains are known for their moss.
Glasgow's glass is well known for its gloss.
But Moscow has glass cows
And Glasgow has moss cows
I guess somehow their cows must have crossed.

Extra Cheese Pizza

When ordering pizza, say, "Please,
I'd like to add on extra cheese.
And when I say extra,
Give such melty pleth'ra
With ease it would stretch overseas.

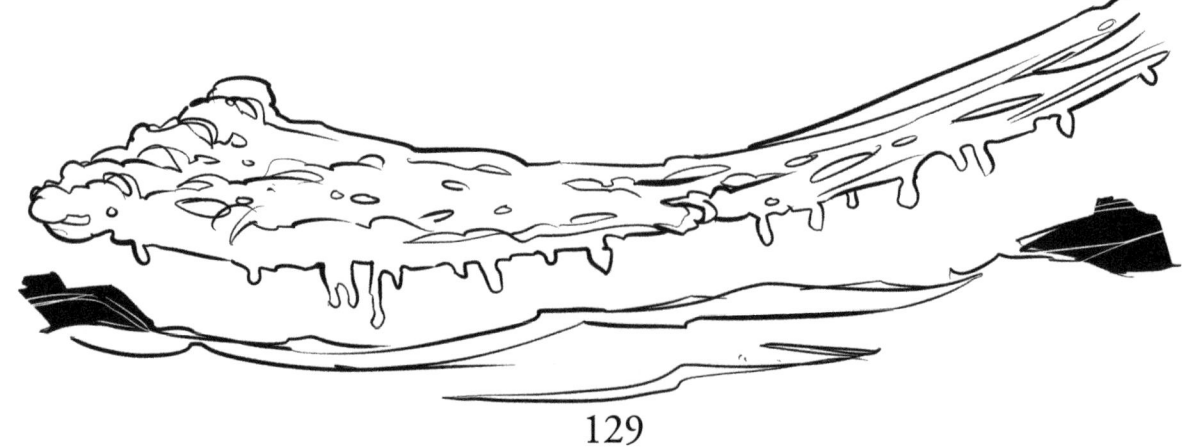

Don't Lick a Cricket

If you ever decide to eat cricket,
It's best to just chew it, don't lick it.
You can stick them on picks
Or just pick them with sticks,
But if this makes you sick, I'd just skip it.

Slurpees

If your goal is a big case of burpies,
What you'll need is a surplus of Slurpees.
Ask the clerk, "Sir, please,
May I have some Slurpees?"
But don't slur, or you may get beef jerkies.

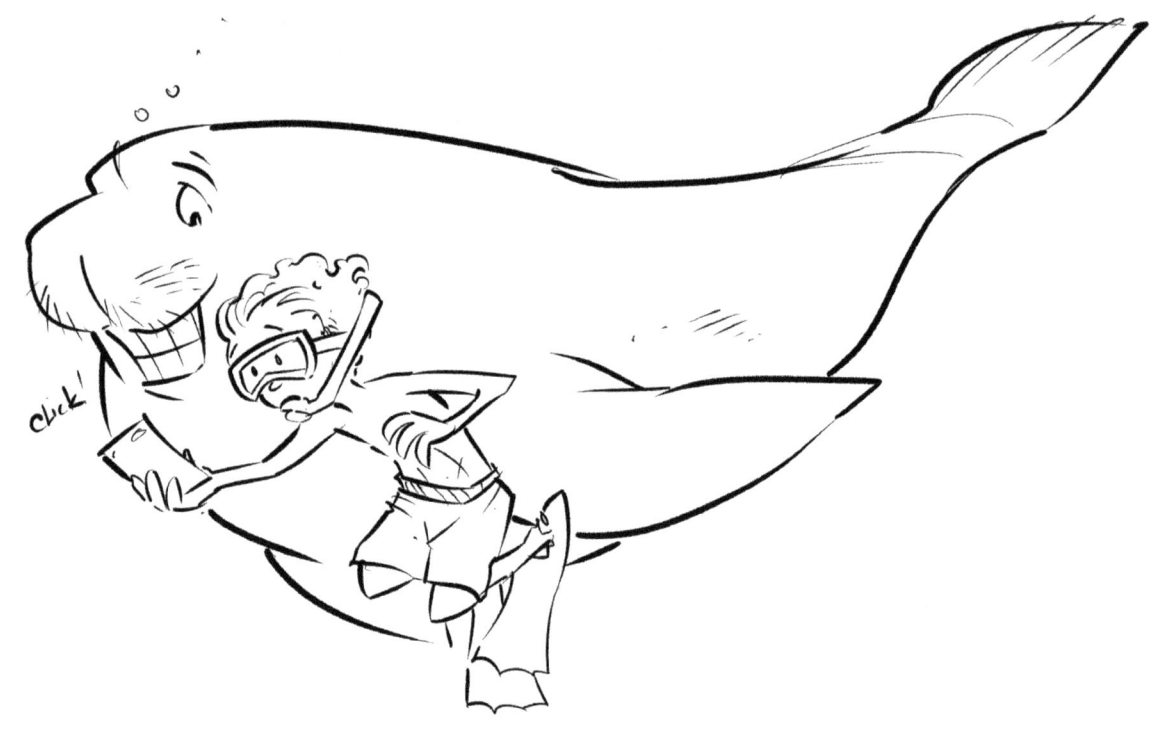

Manatee

Hugh was a friendly old manatee.
If you think that he's mean, that's insanity.
Sure, a grumpy old bull
Could bite off a whole hull
But he's cool for the love of Hugh Manatee!

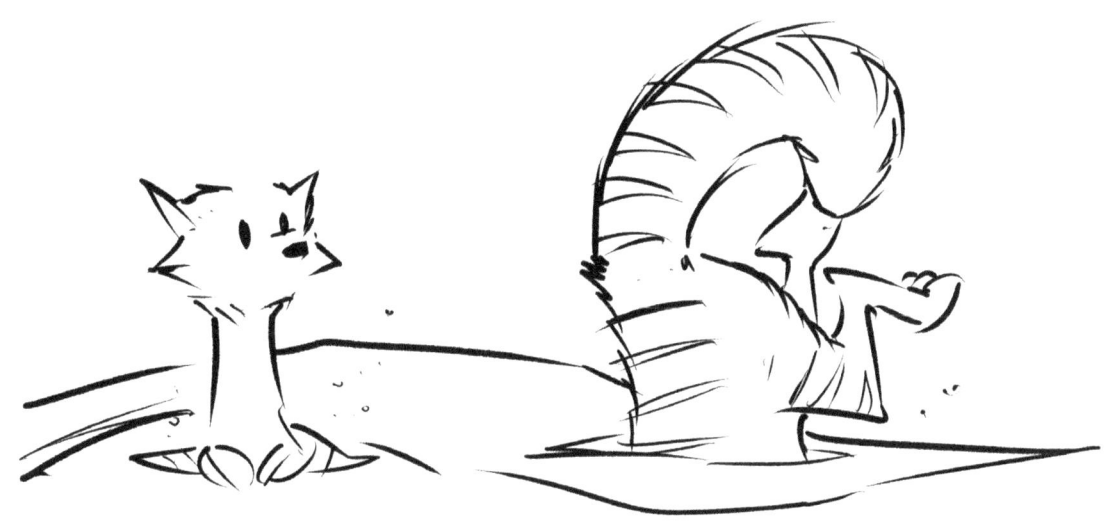

Meerkat

Don't confuse common cats with a meerkat.
They're a specialized mongoose, no mere cat.
In the desert they dwell
Digging tunnels quite well,
And a cat can't do anything near that.

*Phew! You just read all fifty limericks. Great job!
I do have this big blank page here, though. Should
I just leave it blank or should we go for 51? All
right, if you say so!*

BONUS LIMERICK!

Macadamia

There once was a smart macadamia.
Who excelled in all high academia.
If you're wondering: "What?!
How'd that nut make the cut?"
Other nuts don't lack guts, they lack-a-brainia.

What? No More Poems?!

Take a deep breath. It's going to be okay. I would love to show you more poems, but there just aren't enough pages for them.

But guess what? I have more hilarious, exclusive poems just for you that I posted on my website at DerekTaylorKent.com/HysphericalRhymes.

You can also sign up for my super-fun Fan Club there and be the first to know when I have new books and poems coming out, plus get lots of other cool stuff like free coloring pages and lesson plans for teachers.

I hope that you've learned a lot about poetry and that you're inspired to write some of your own. If you do, I can't wait to read it!

You can send me a poem at the same website and I'll be posting my favorites for all my fans to see, so your poem can get really famous, plus you can call yourself a published poet!

Remember at the beginning when I gave you the challenge of writing down your favorite rhymes? To give you a head start on your first poem, try taking those words and come up with new rhymes for them and incorporate them into your poem. I can't wait to see that!

This is where I must bid you adieu, and remind you that there are absolutely, positively, no more…

Okay, okay just one more poem.

I thank you for reading this book.
I'm happy you gave it a look.
If you hated it, please never tell me.
I'd cry for so long, they might sell me.

ABOUT THE AUTHOR

Derek Taylor Kent is the author of 17 books. His best-selling, award-winning titles are treasured in homes across the world, including the wildly popular *Scary School* series, *El Perro con Sombrero*, *The Grossest Picture Book Ever*, *Dinosaur Derby*, *Principal Mikey*, and many more. Derek has been obsessed with reading and writing poetry since he was ten years old and is ecstatic to finally share some of his favorite compositions with the world in *Hysterical Rhymes and How You Can Rhyme Too!* He and his wife, author Sheri Fink, are the founders of Whimsical World, an empowering children's brand that publishes books and produces whimsical merchandise, inspiring entertainment, and magical experiences for children of all ages. For more information, please visit www.WhimsicalWorldBooks.com and www.DerekTaylorKent.com.

ABOUT THE ILLUSTRATOR

Travis Hanson is an Eisner nominated illustrator and has been writing and illustrating comics, books, and games for the last 25 years. His works include the *Bean*, *Tanner Jones and the Quest for the Monkey Stone*, and the current webcomic *Life of the Party*. He resides in So Cal with his wife, 5 kids, 2 son-in-laws, 1 daughter-in-law and a bunch of grandkids. Travis's focus is on creating good and fun art to be enjoyed by all. For more information please visit www.beanleafpress.com.

CPSIA information can be obtained
at www.ICGtesting.com
Printed in the USA
LVHW020121020222
709845LV00003B/19